THIS BOOK BELONG TO ....

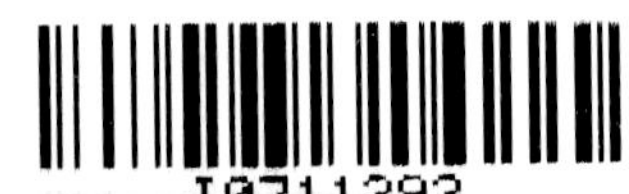

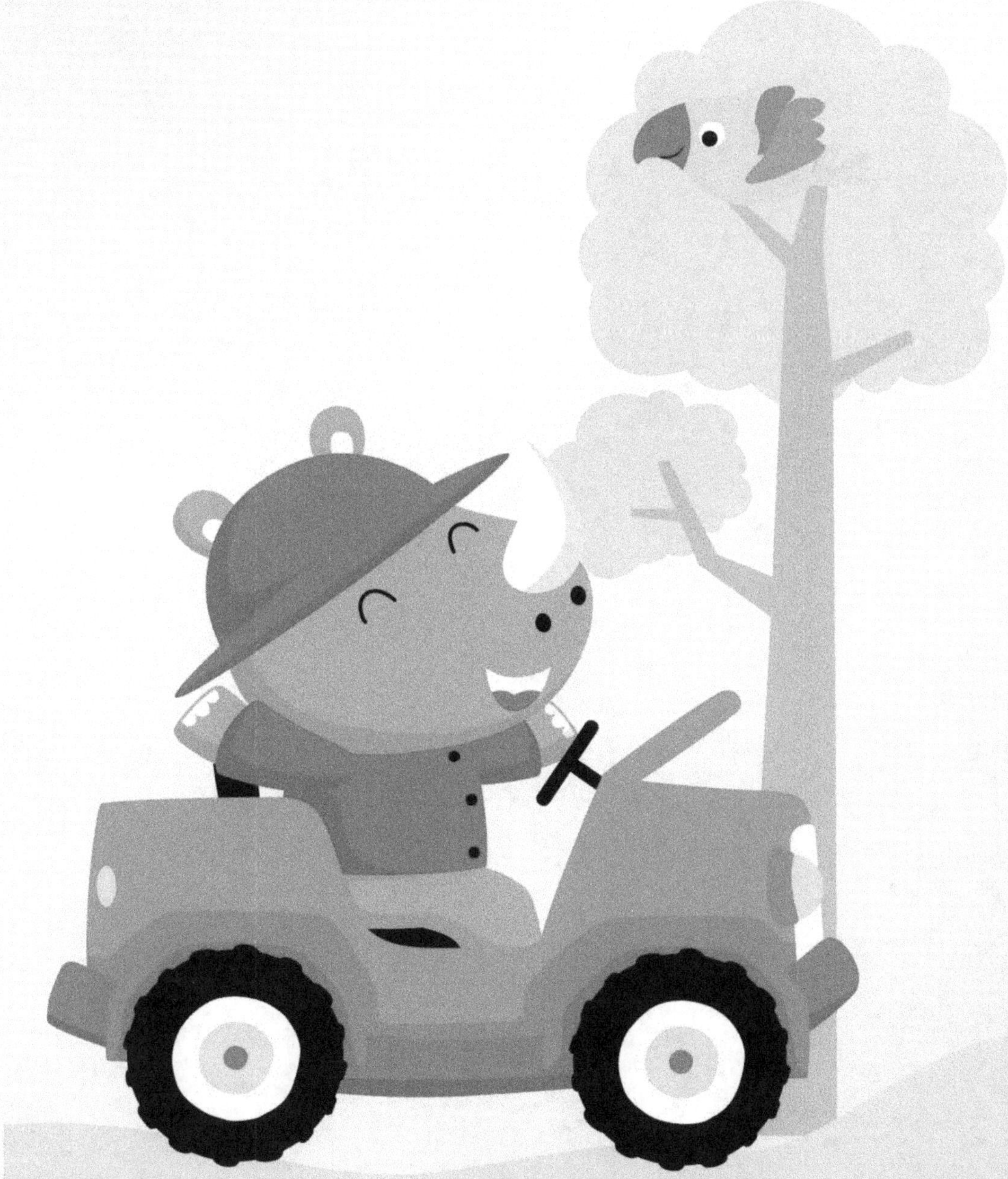

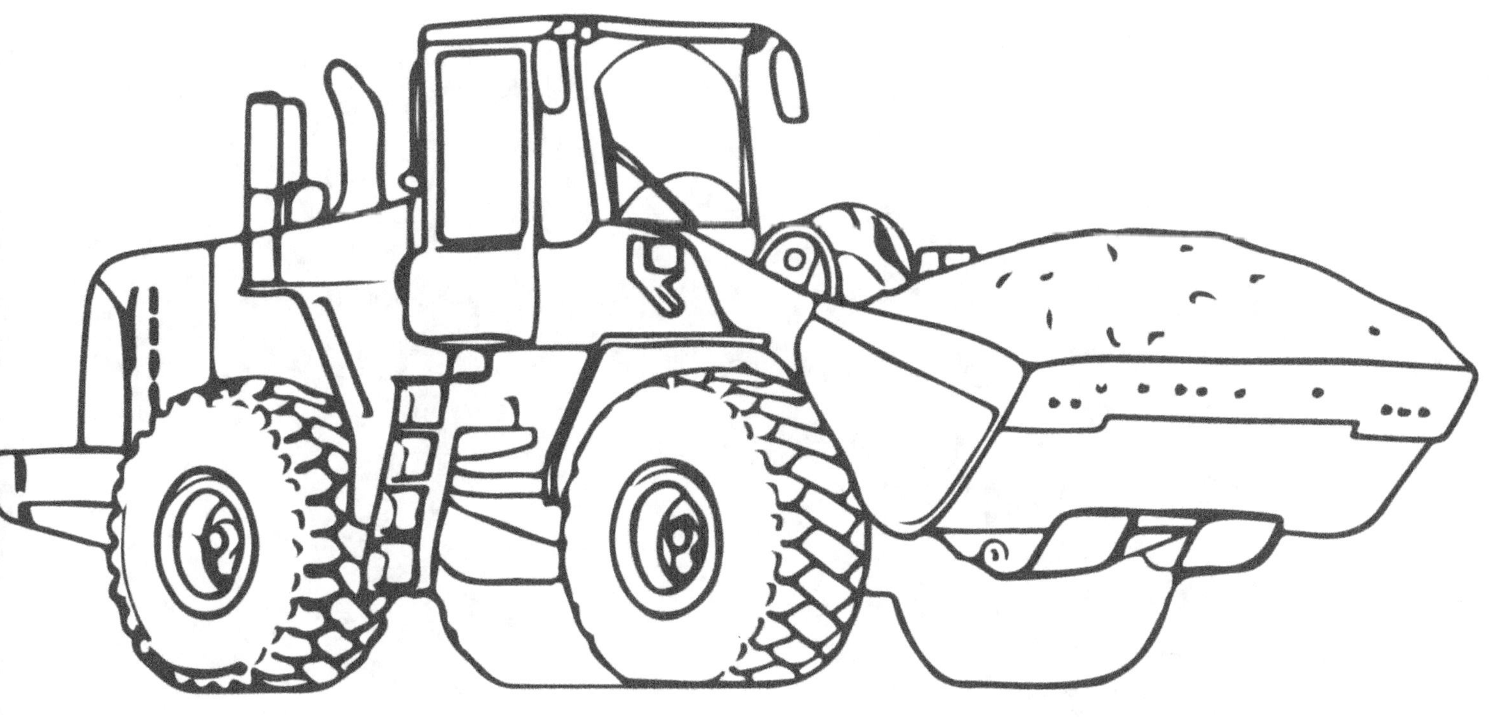

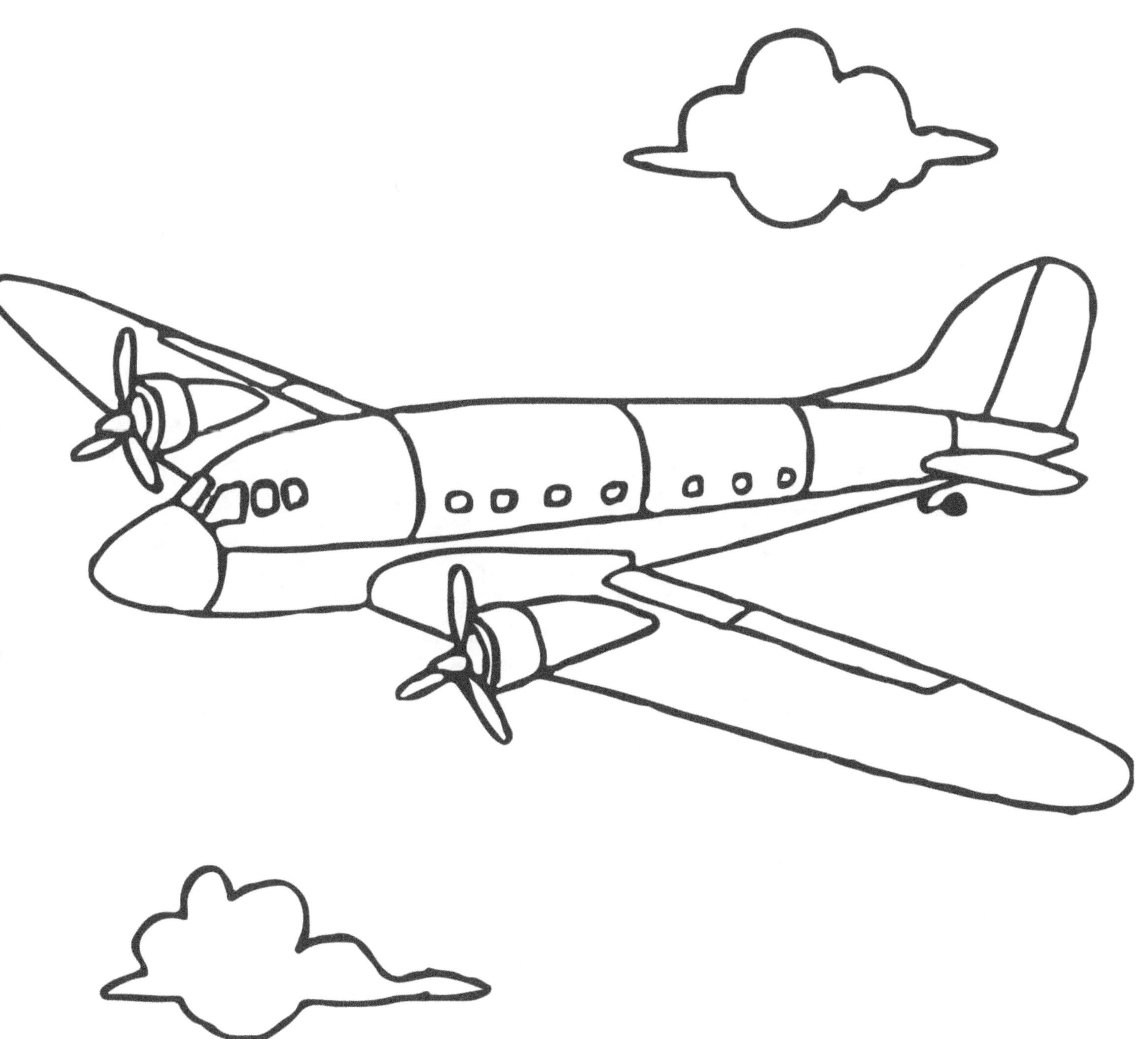

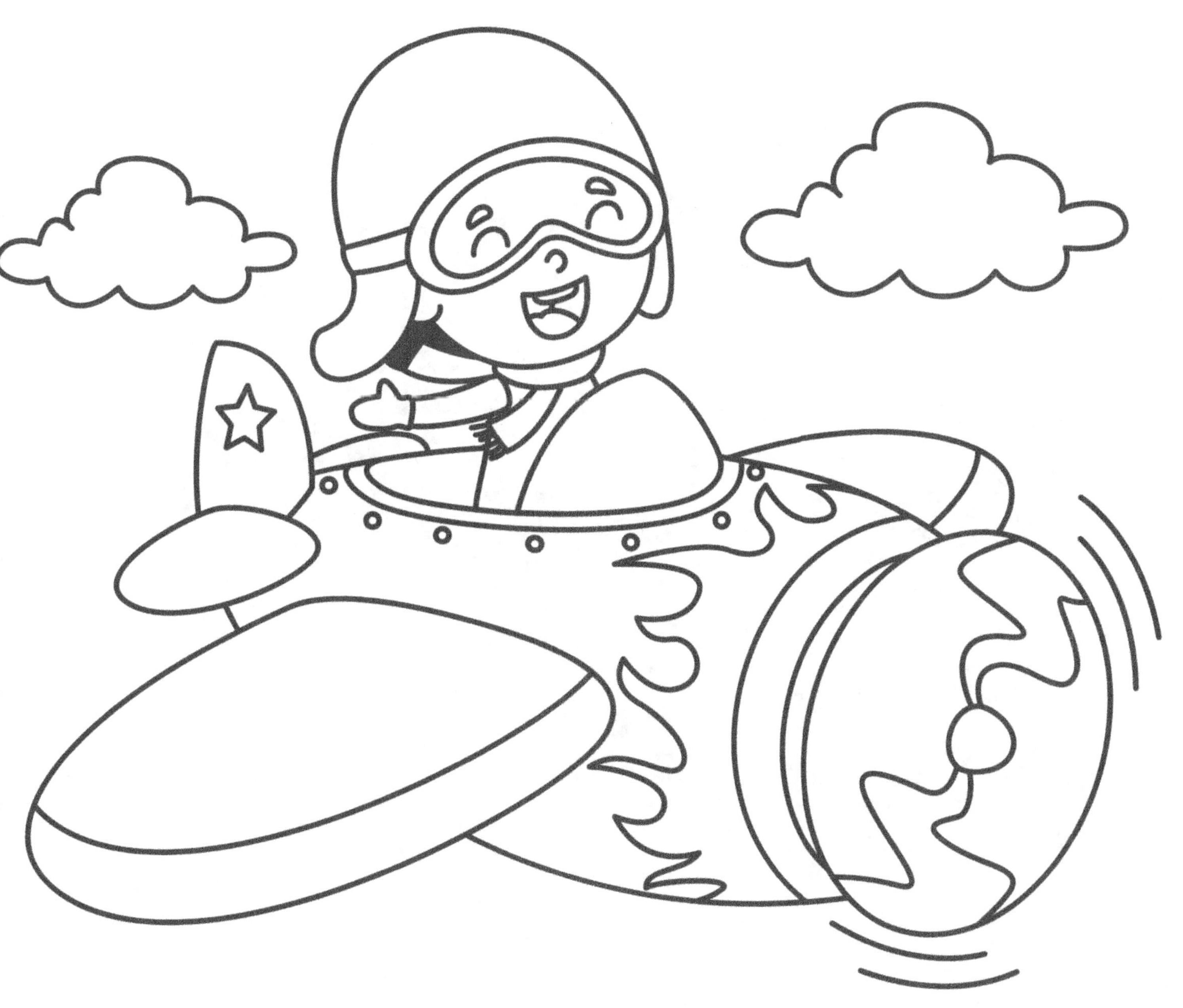

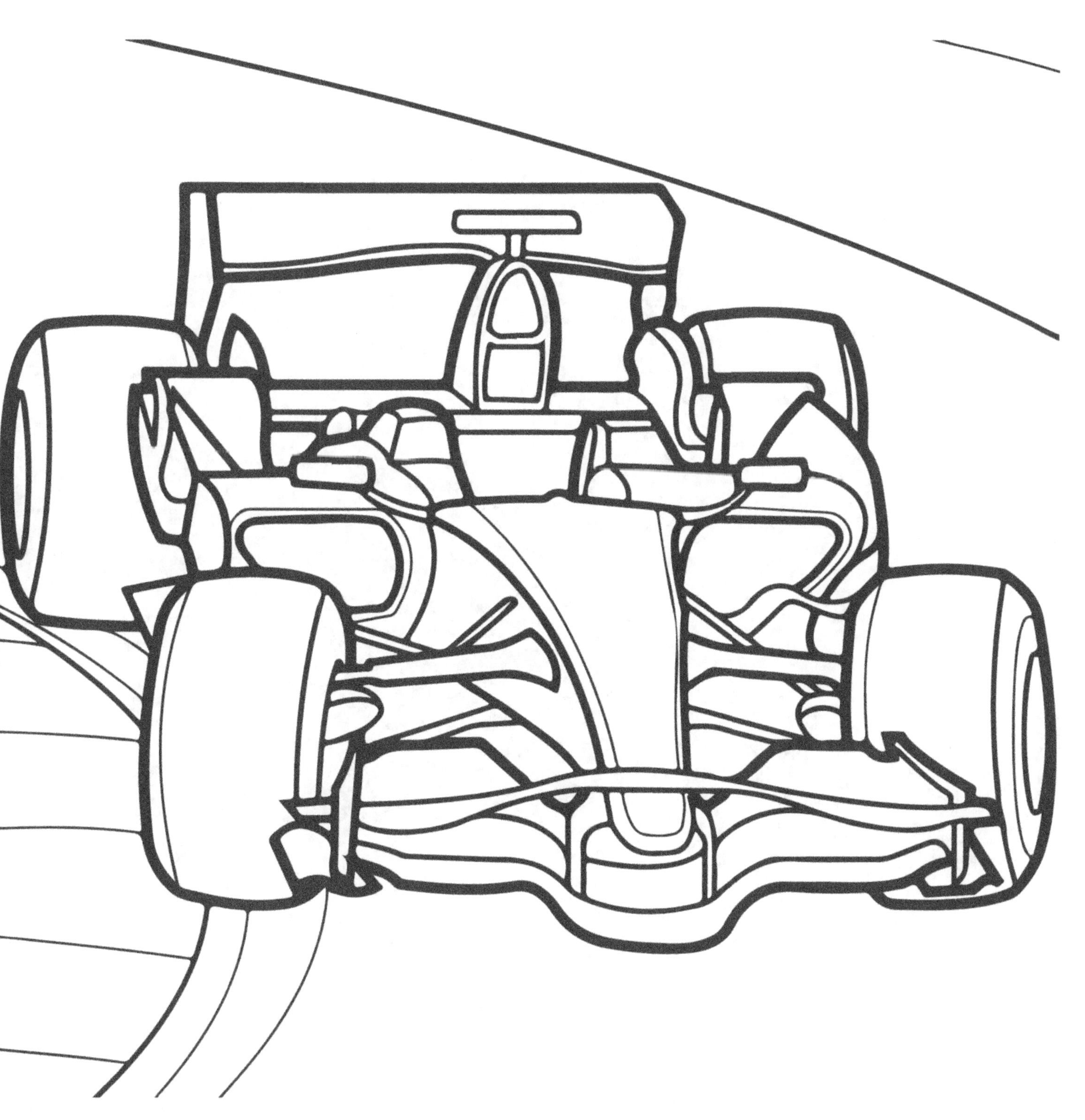

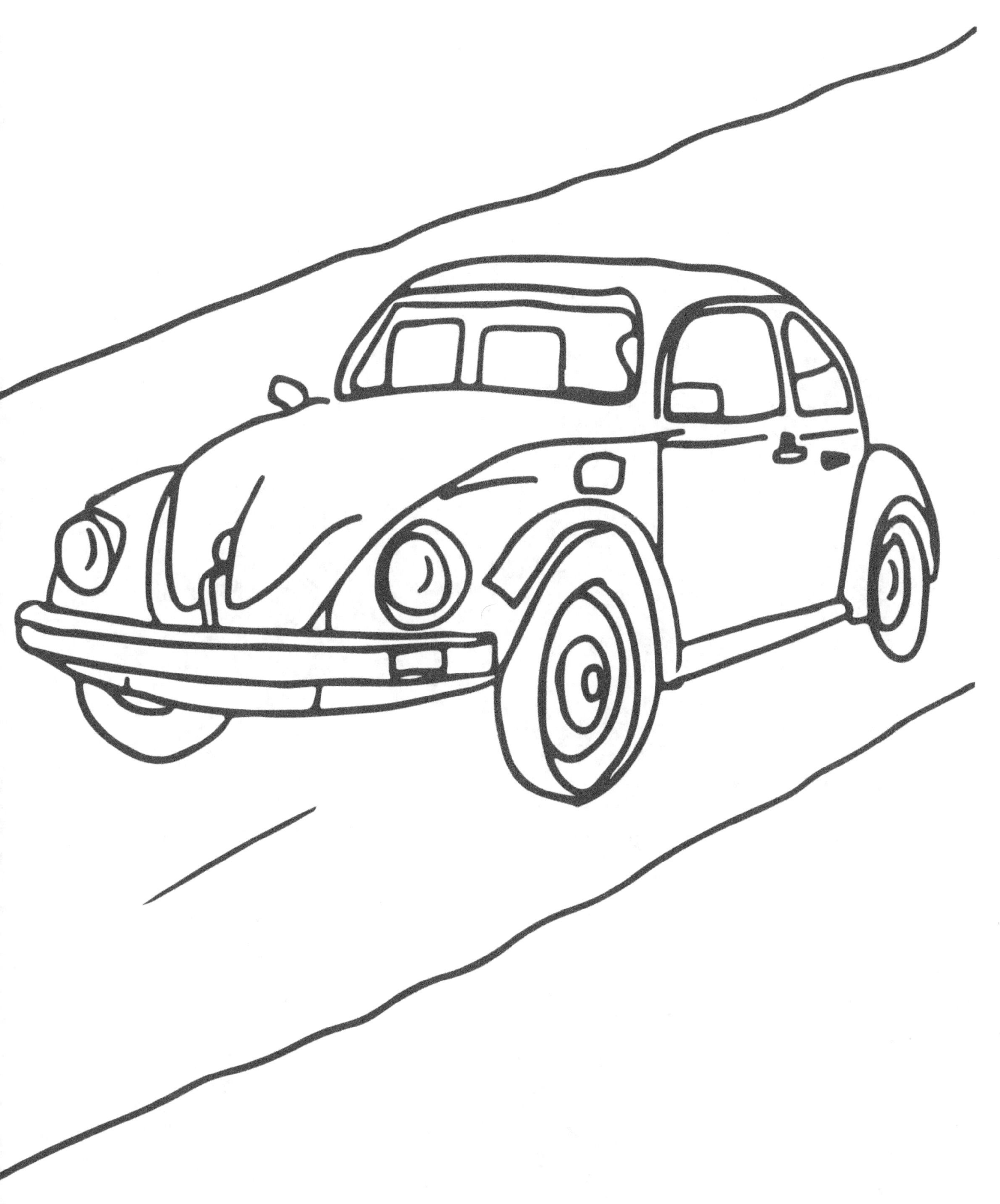

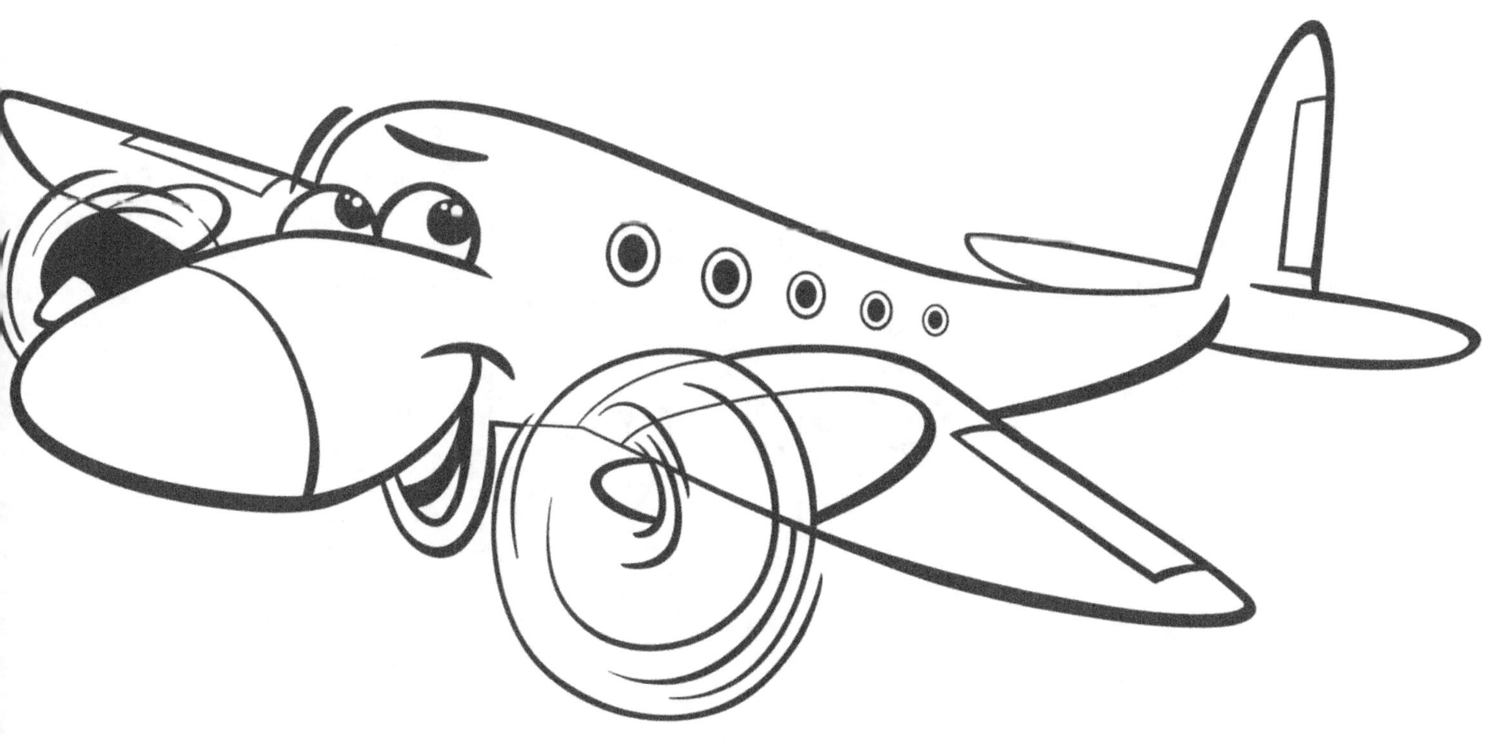

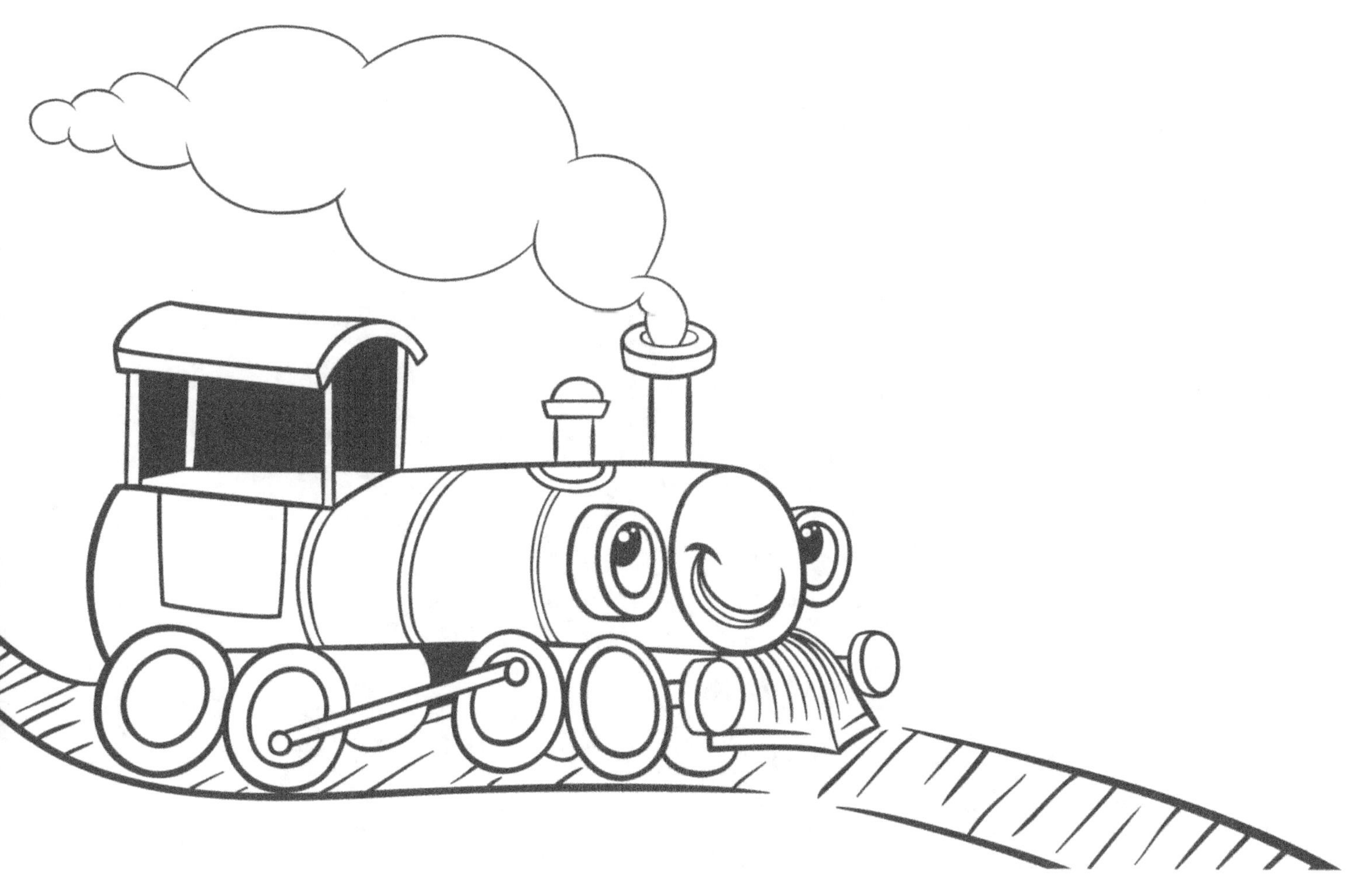

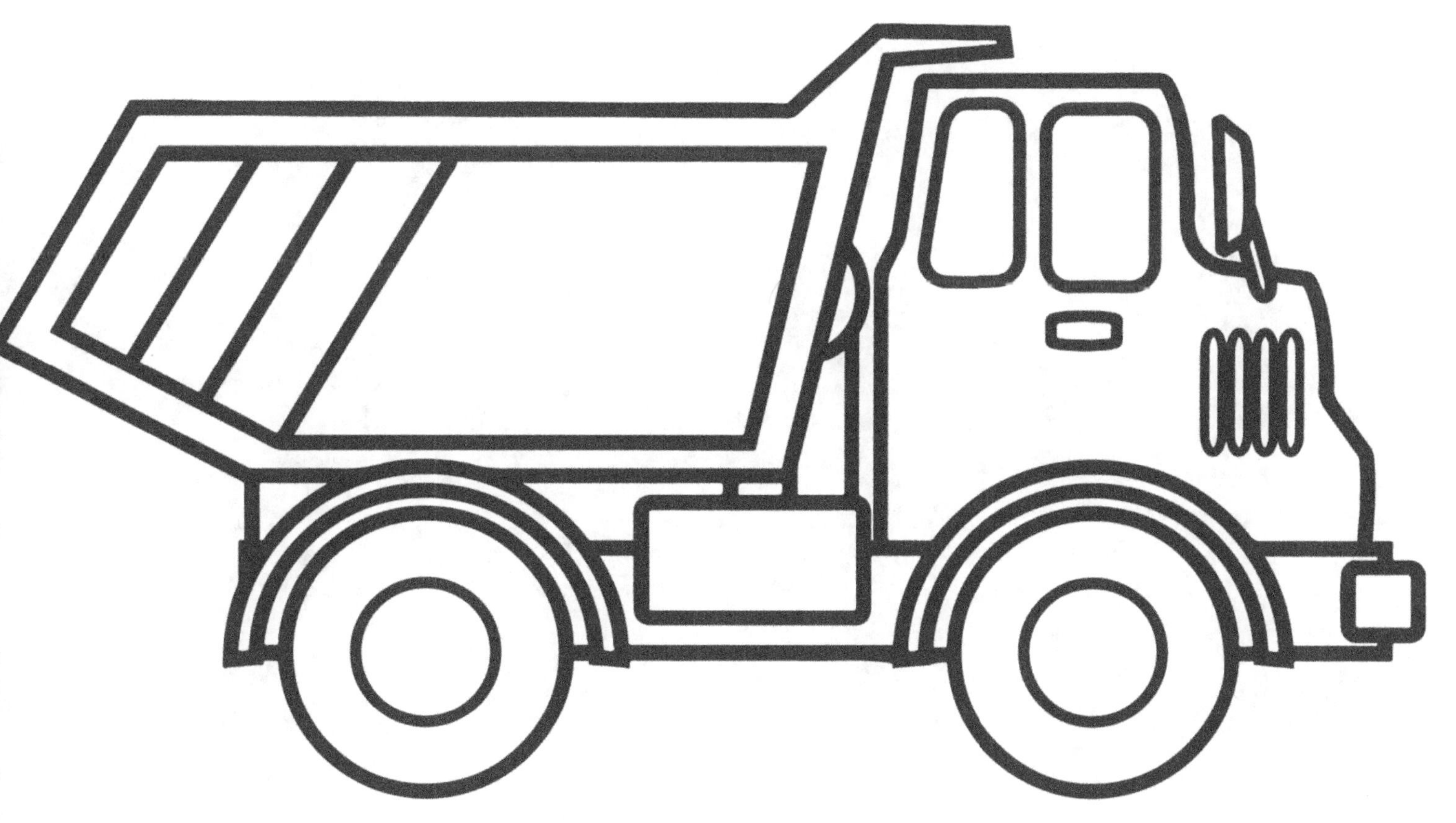

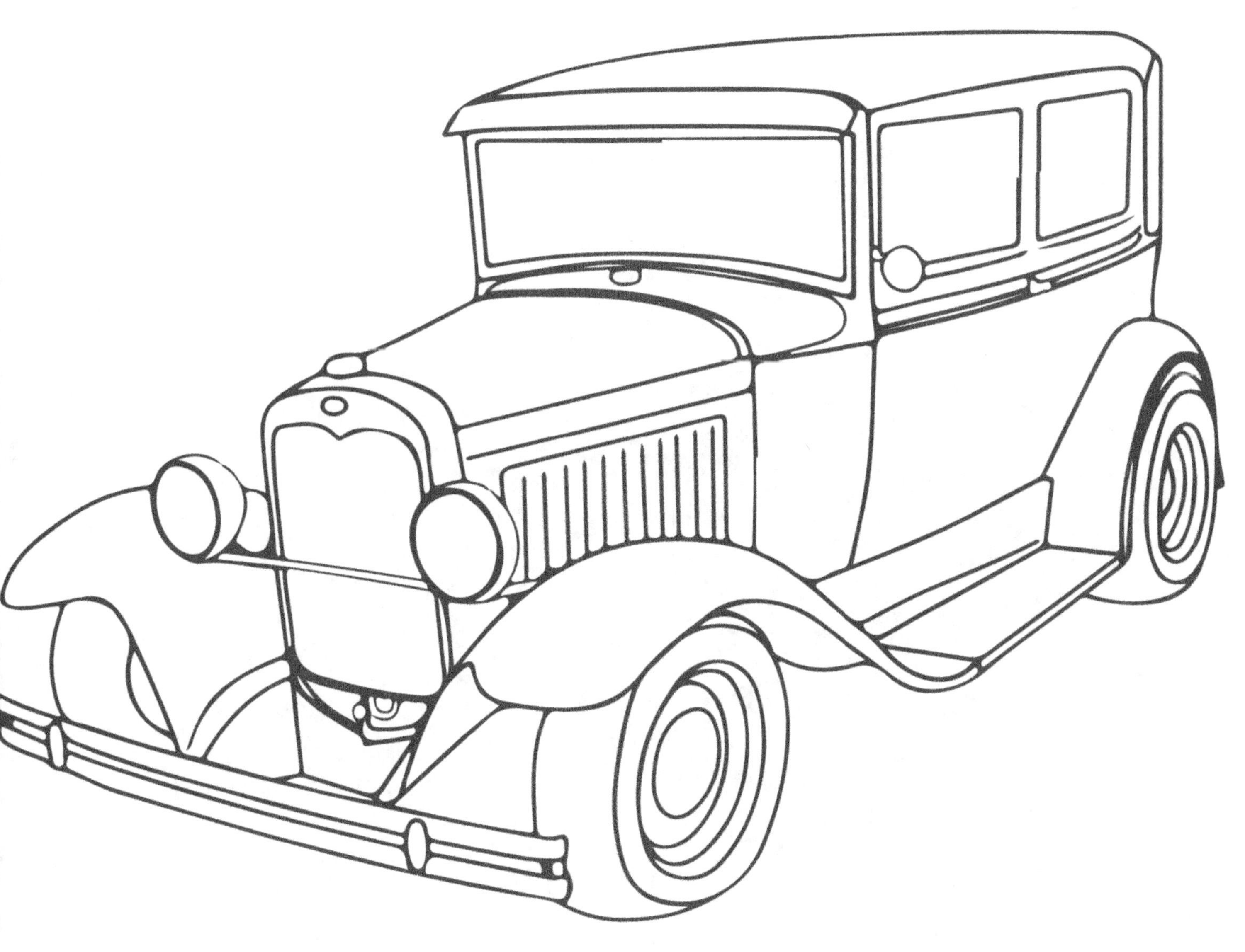

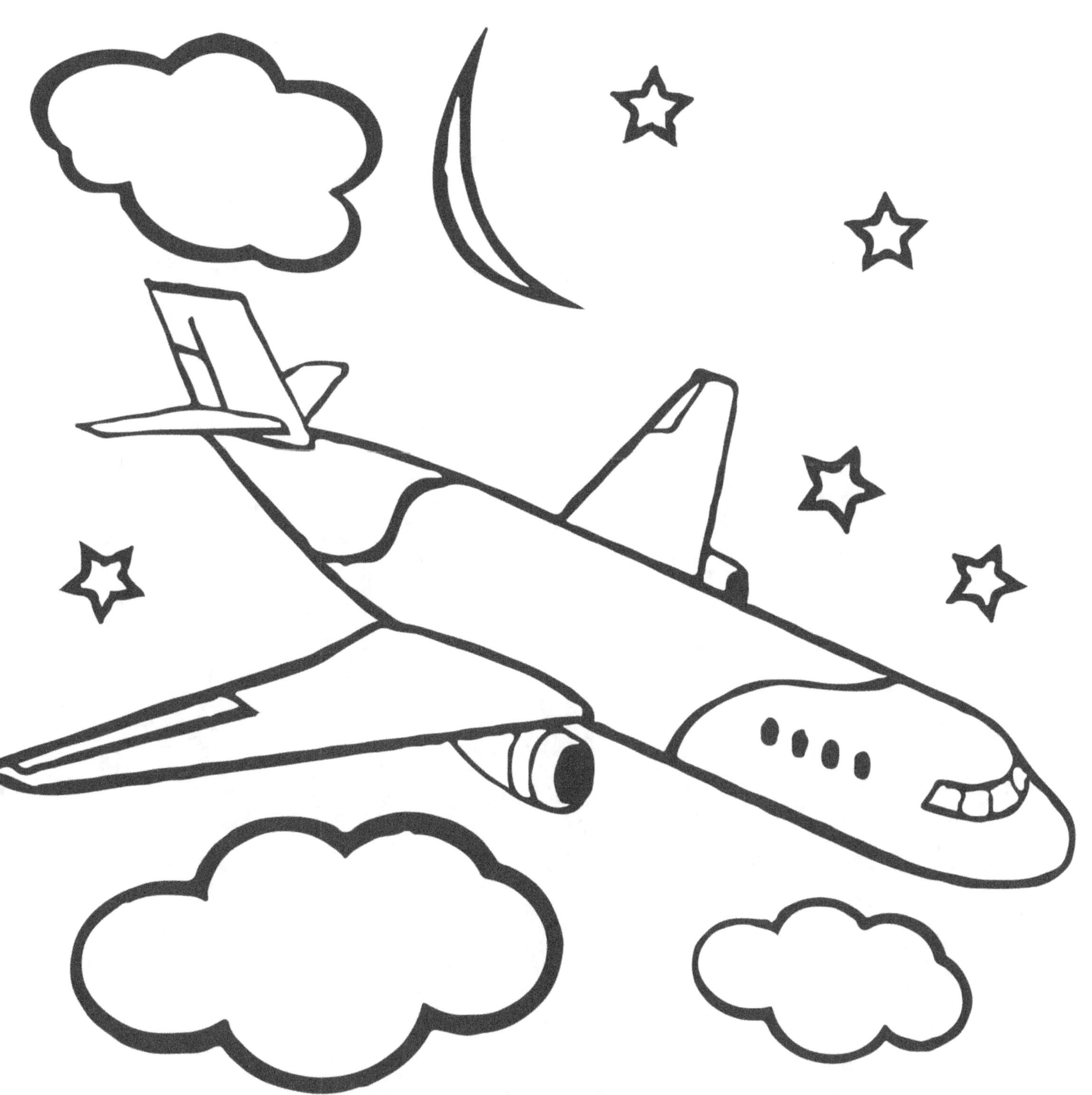

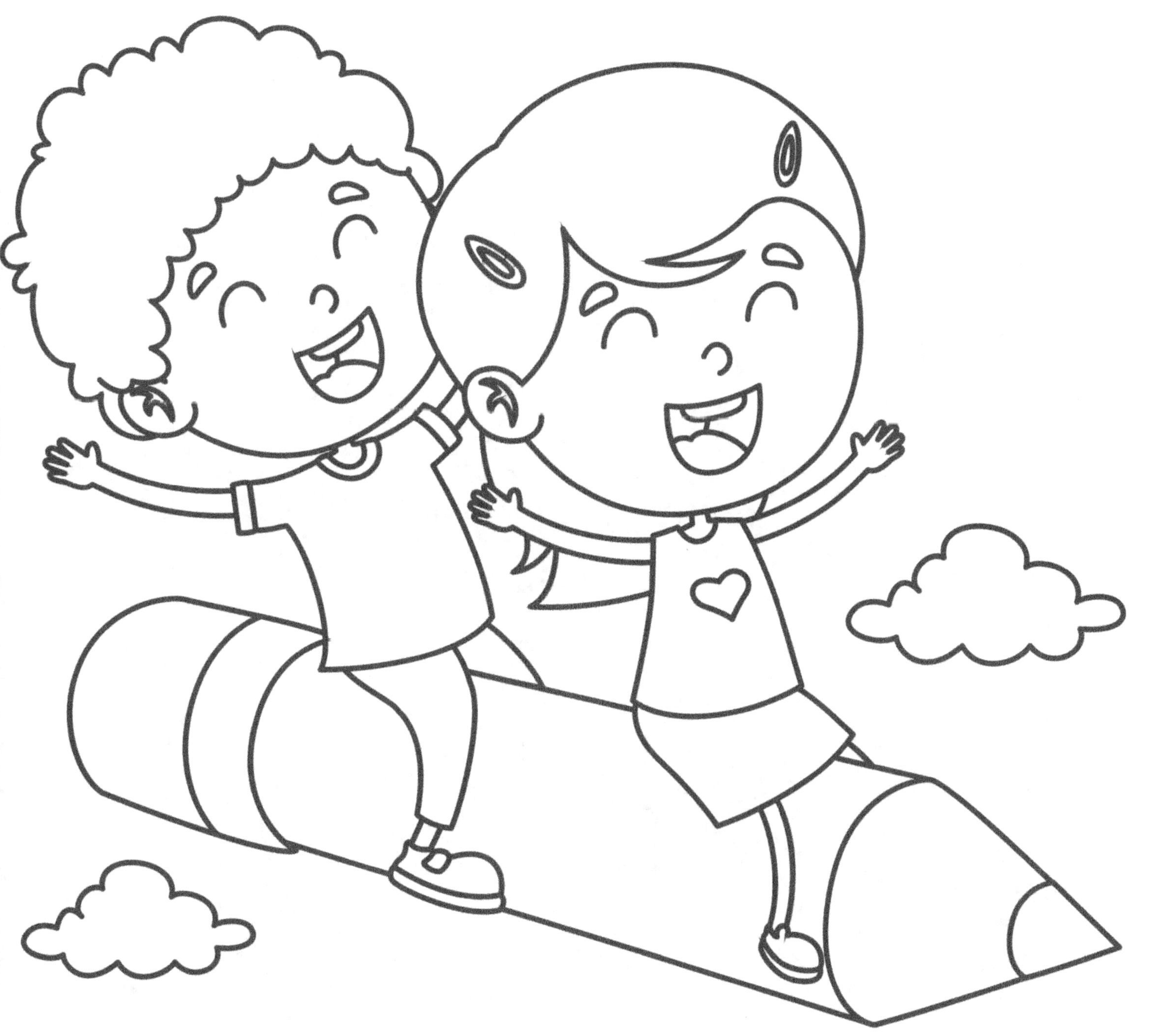

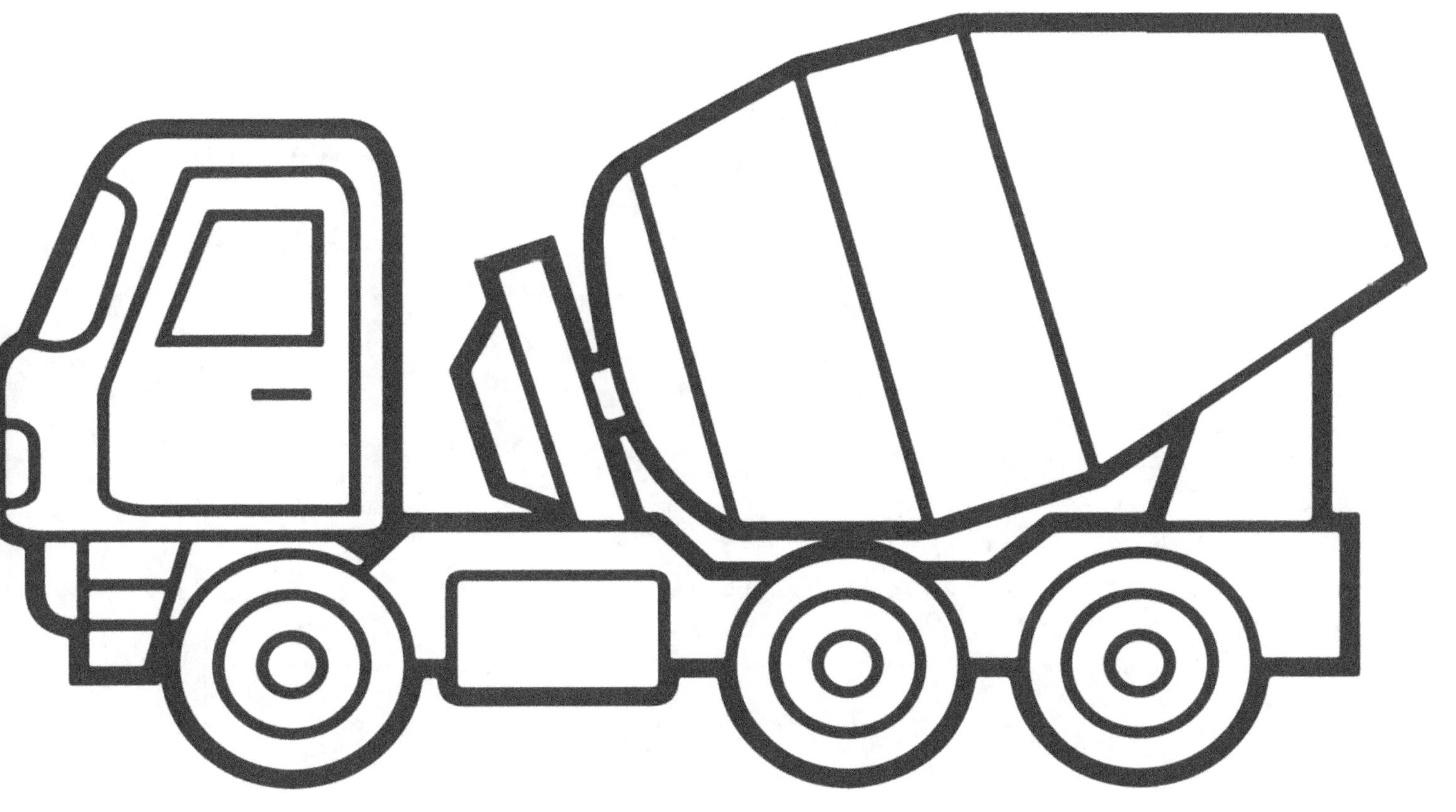

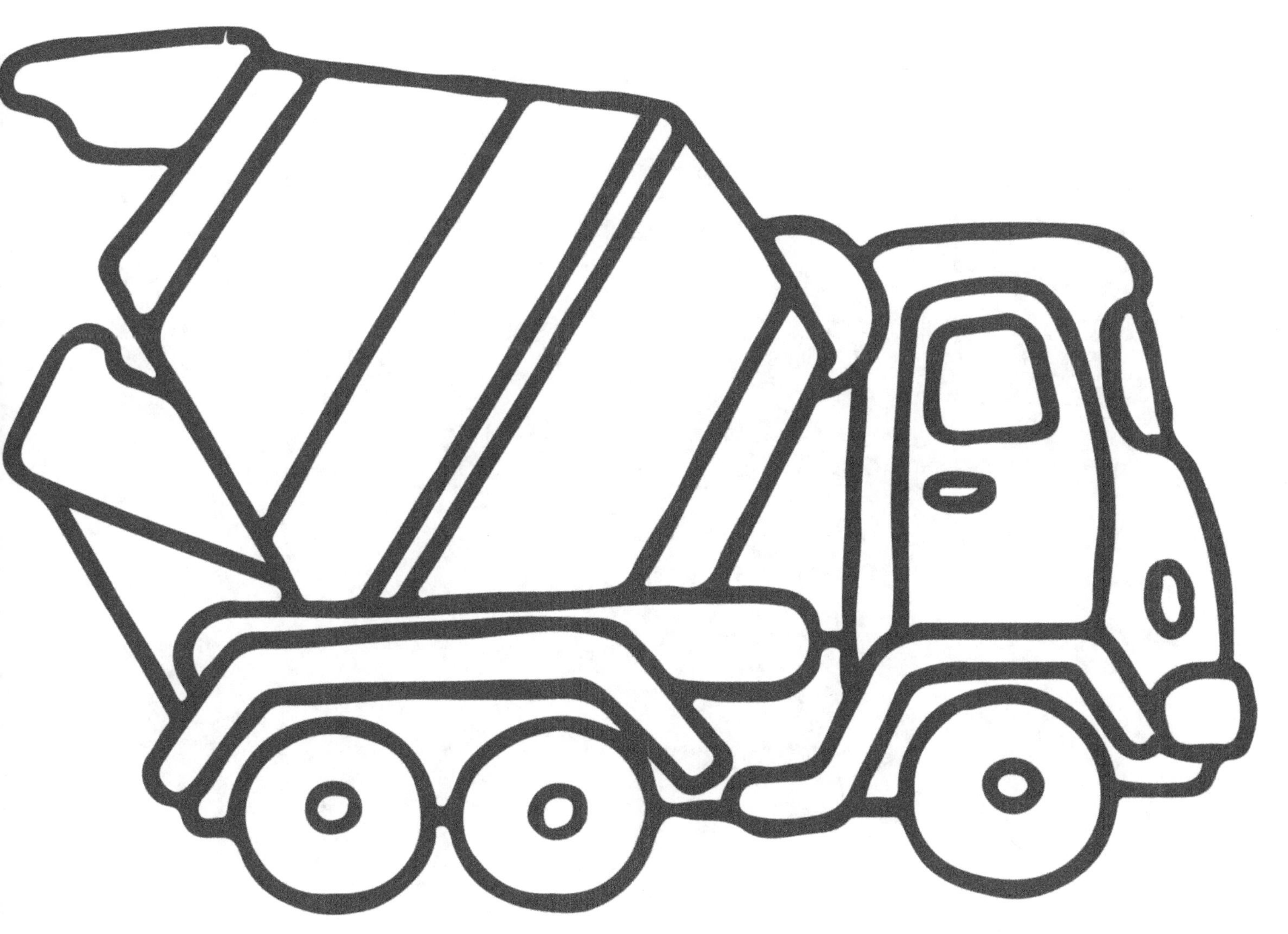

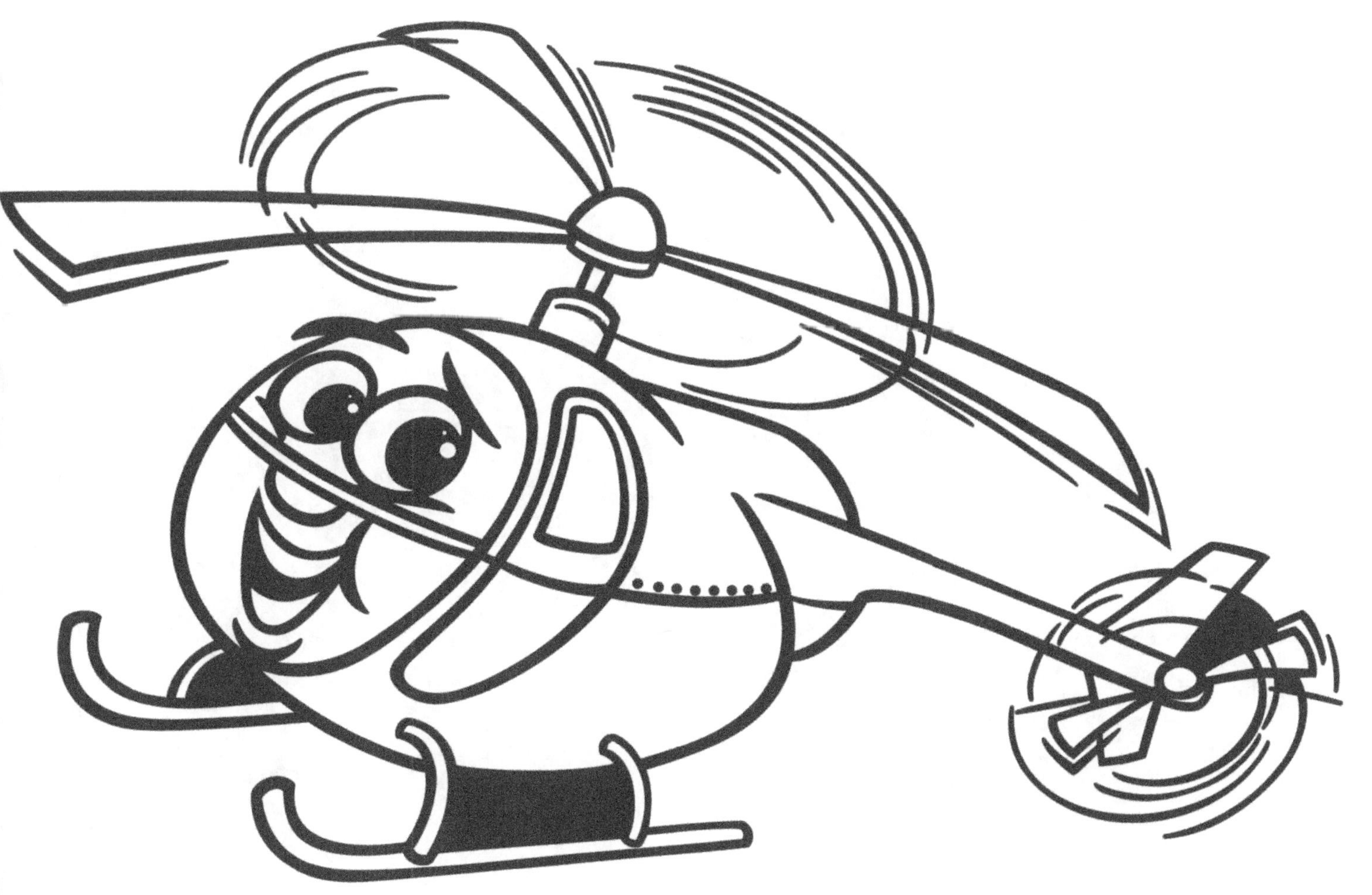

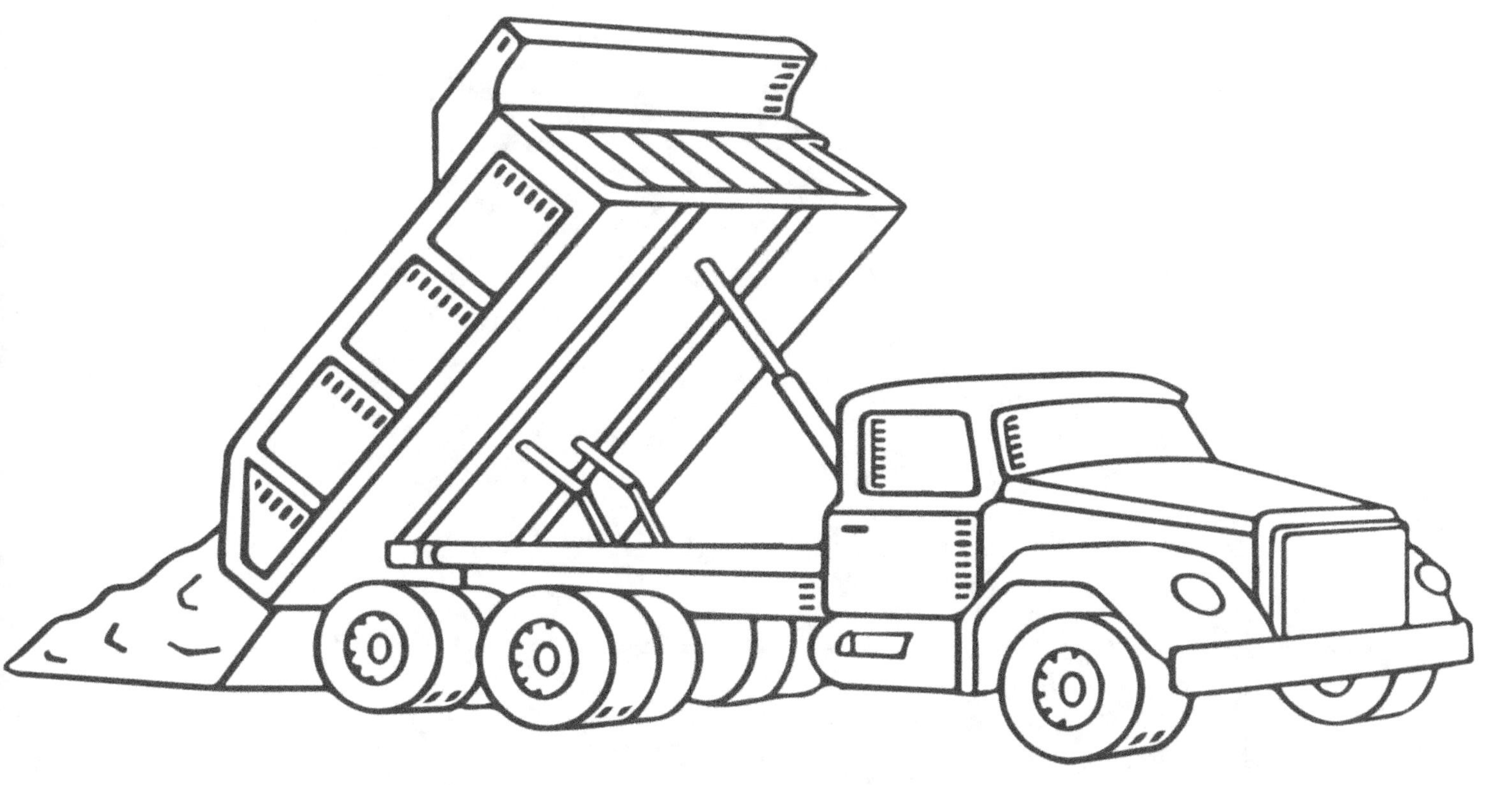

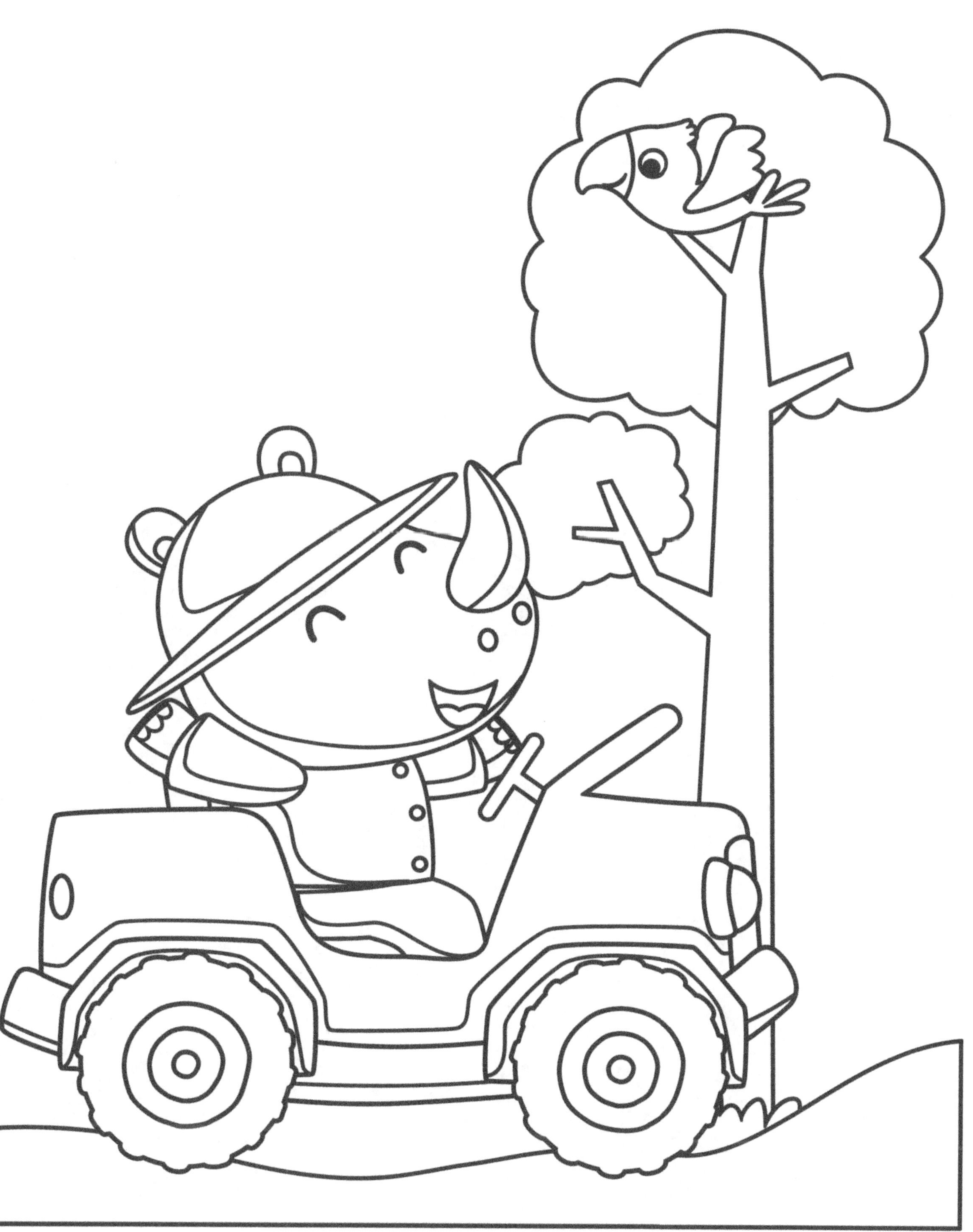

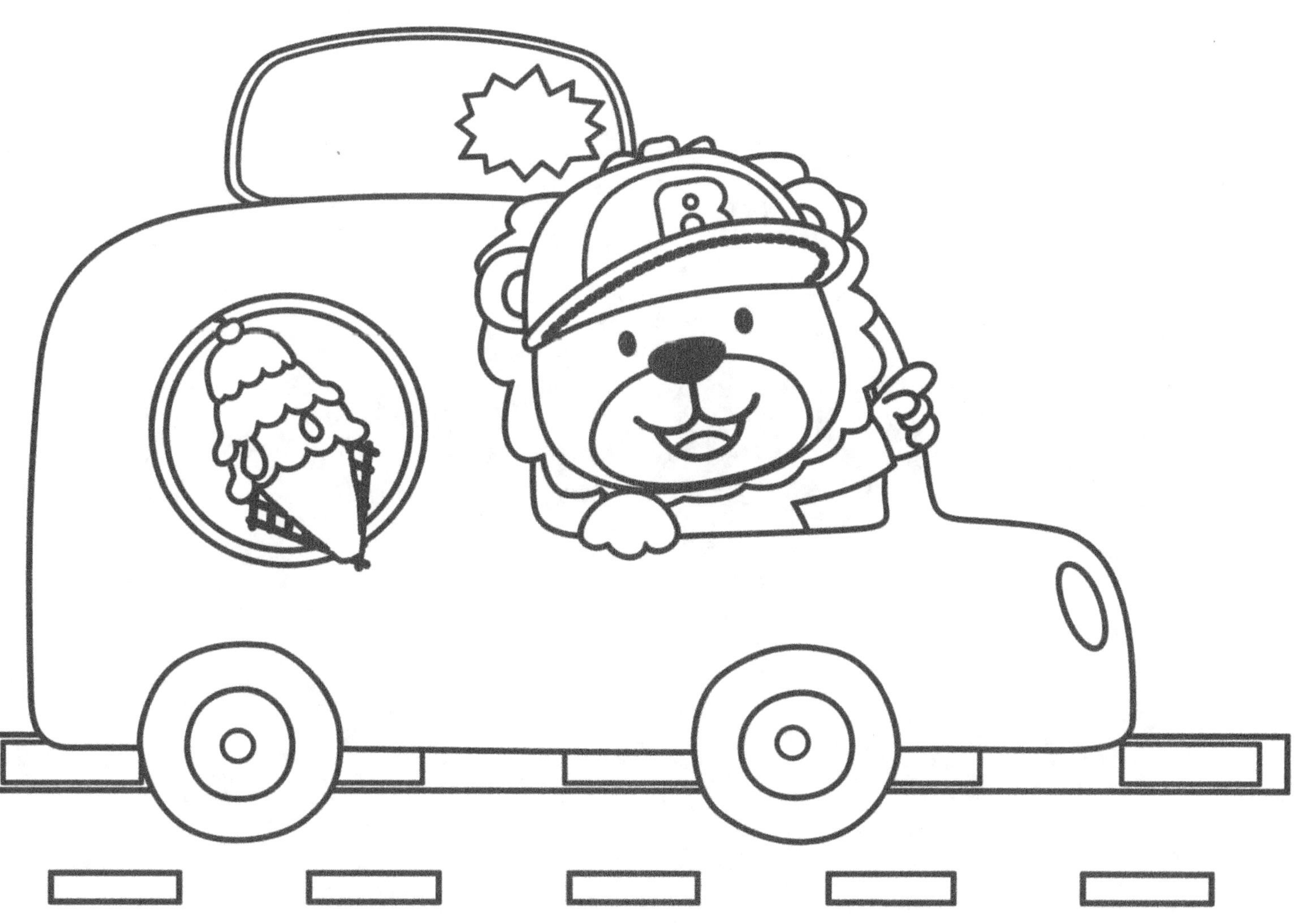

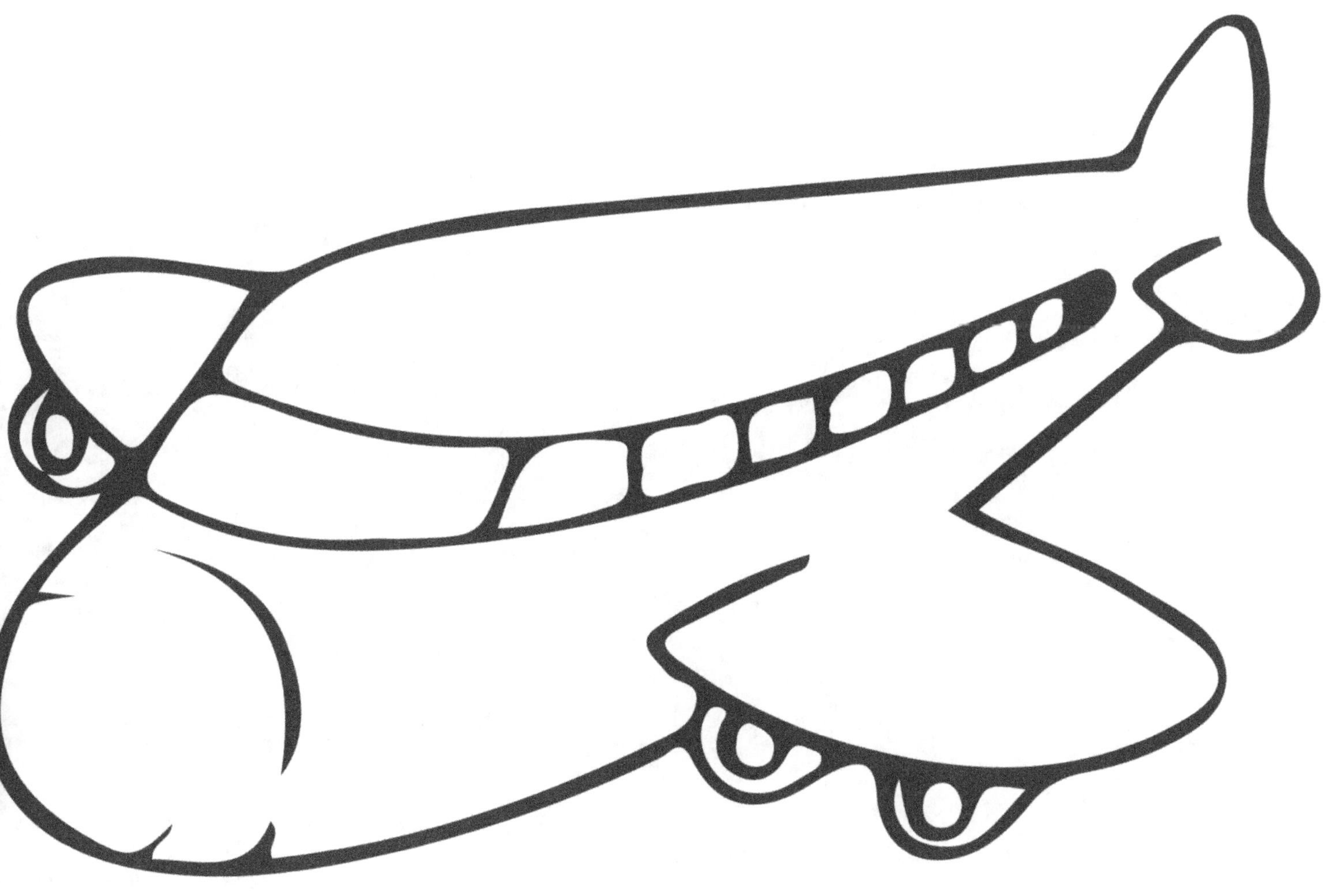

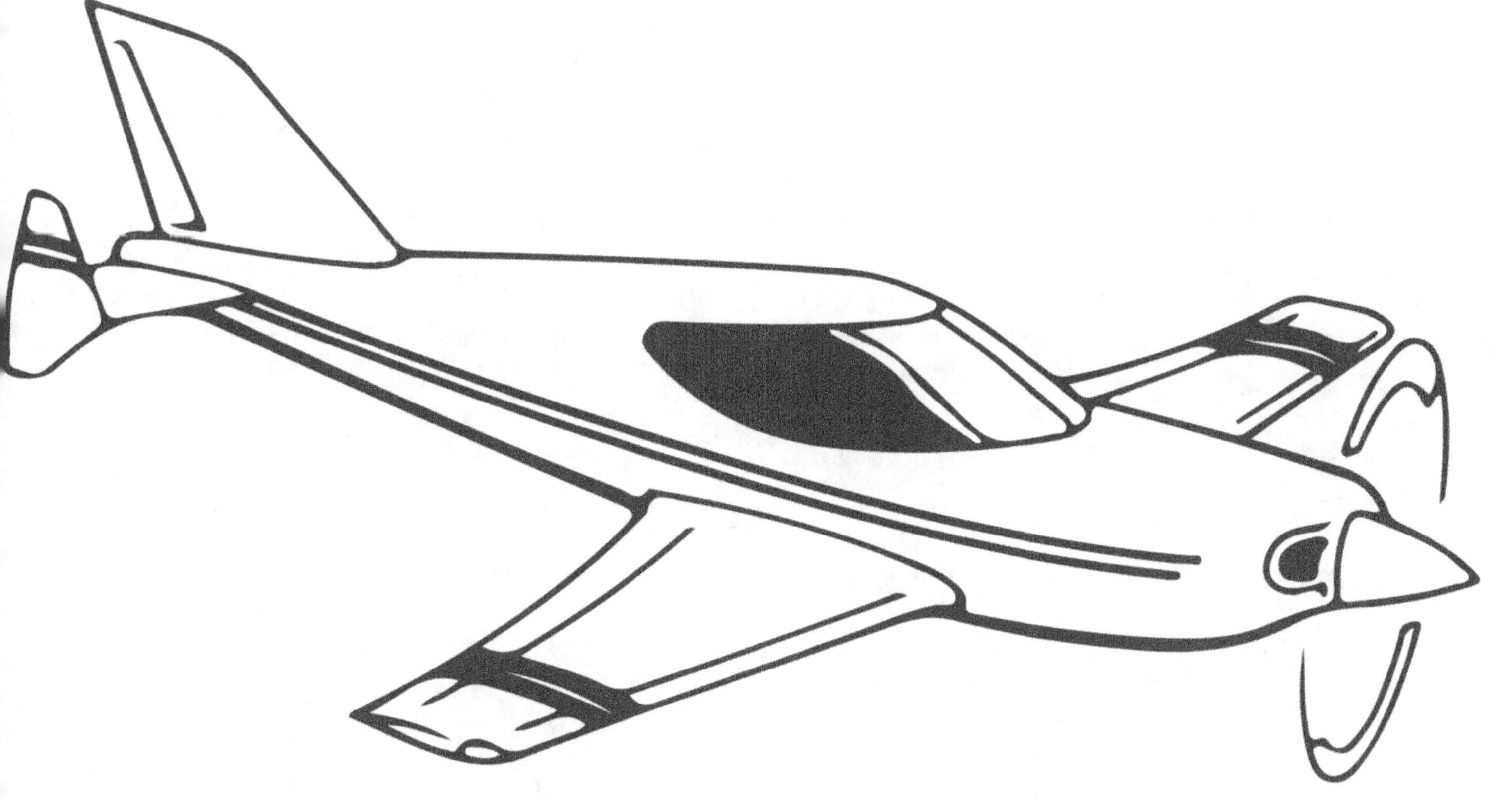

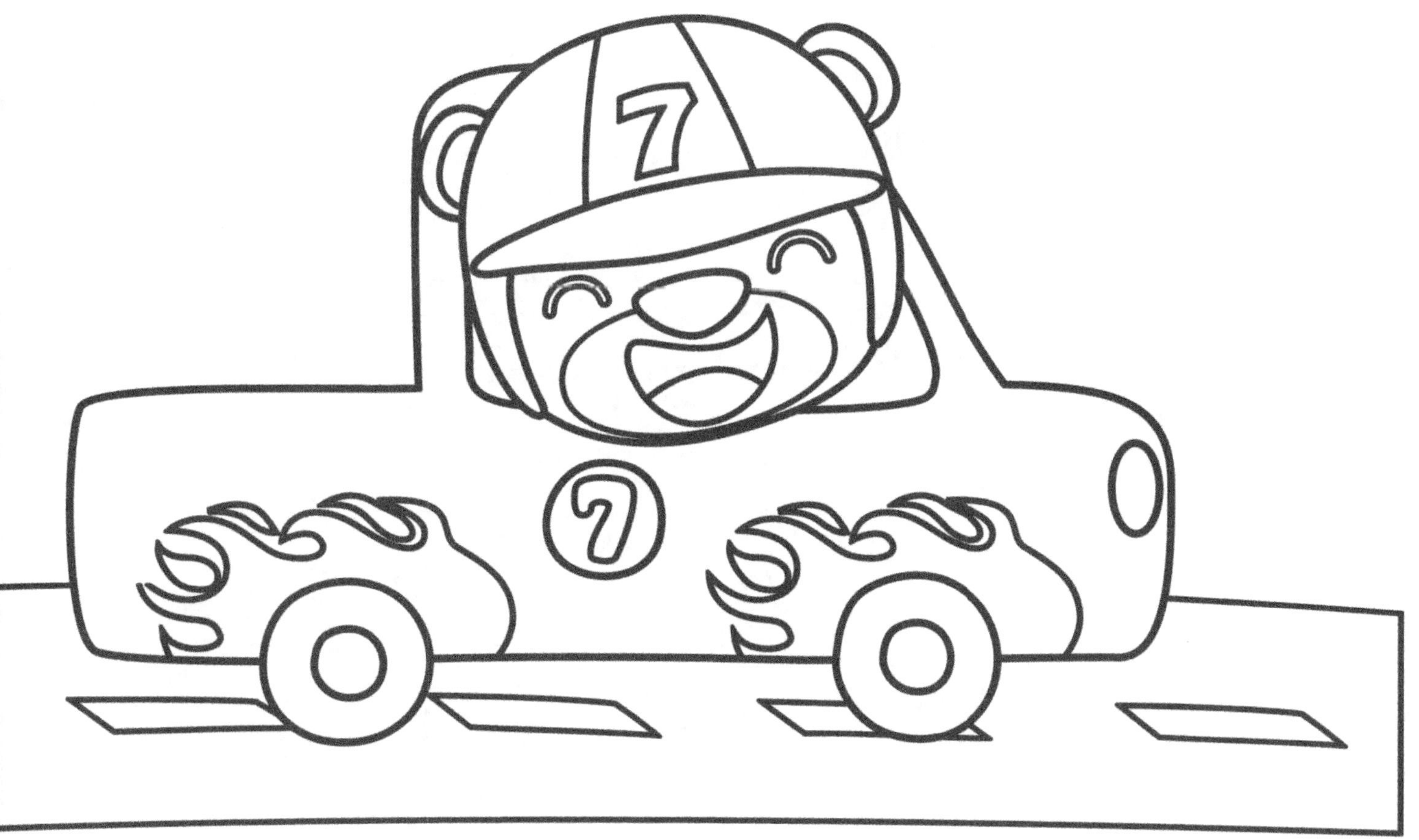

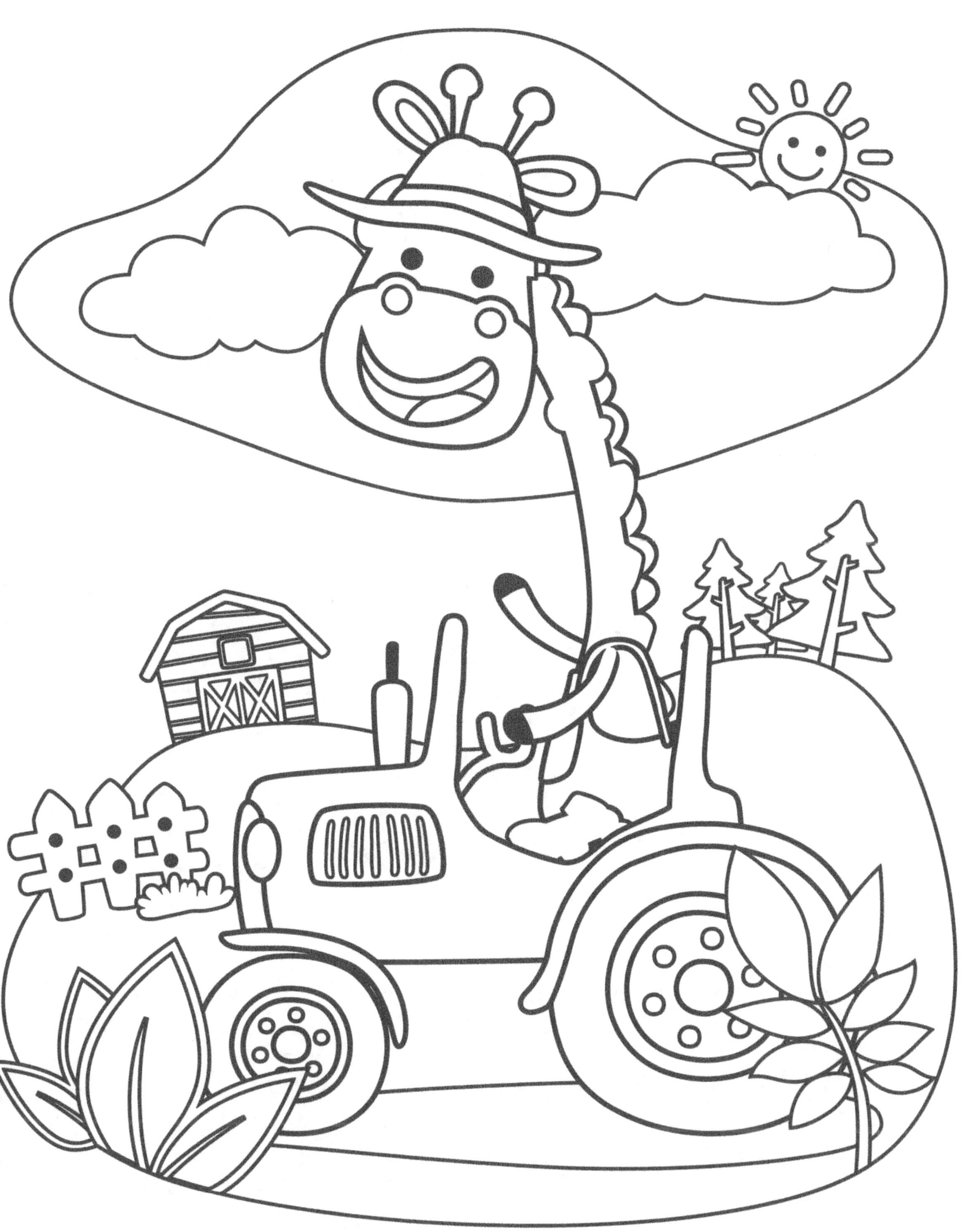

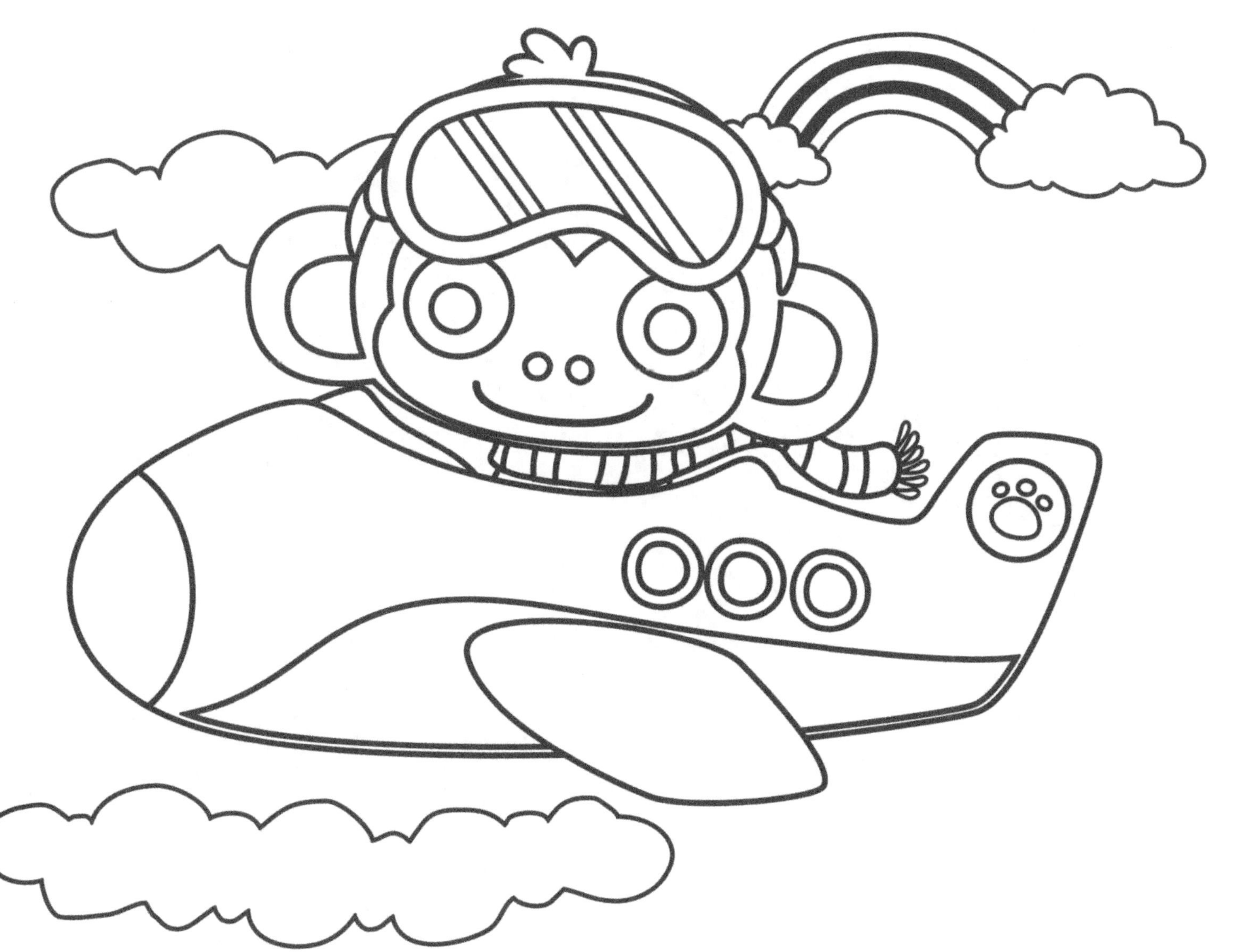

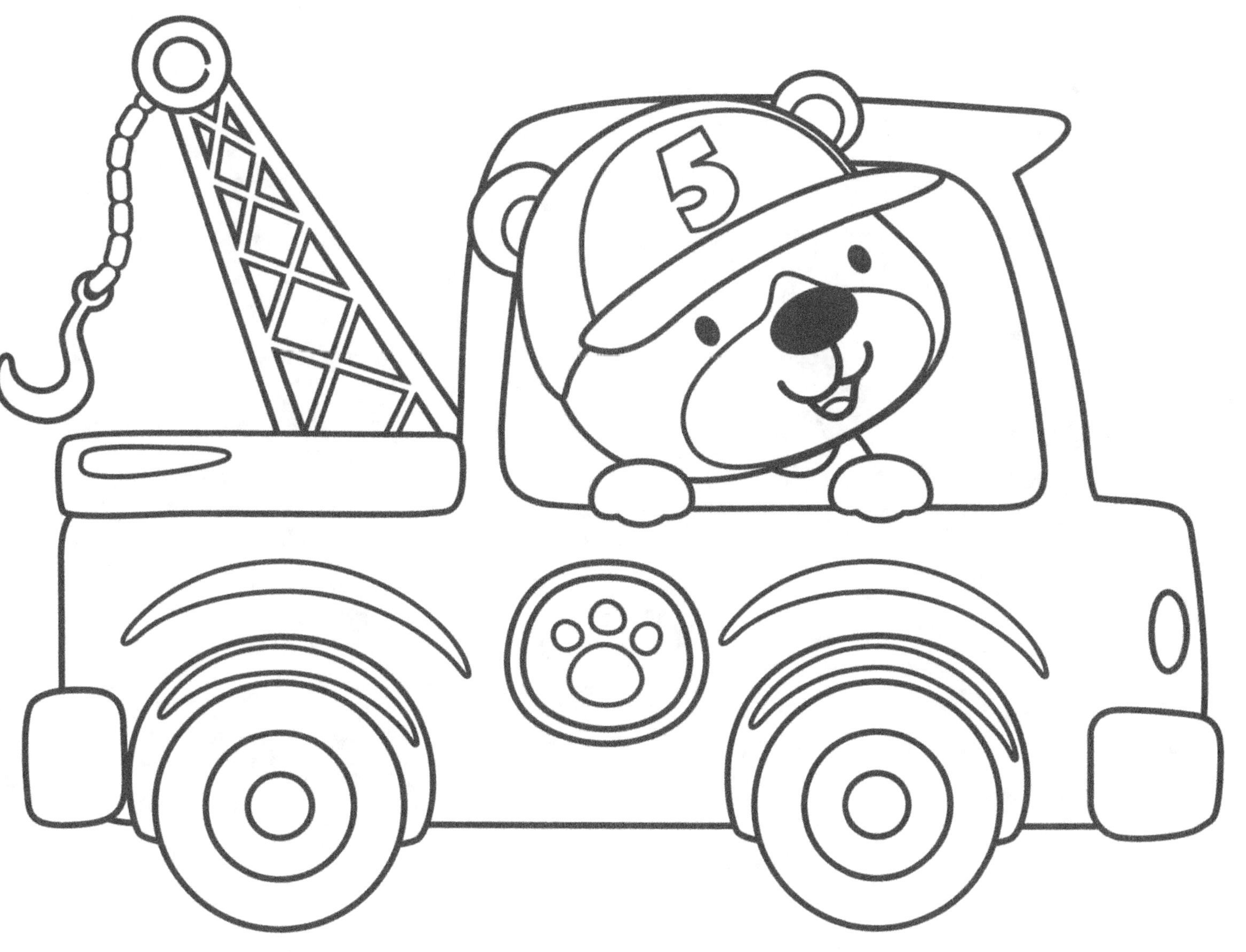

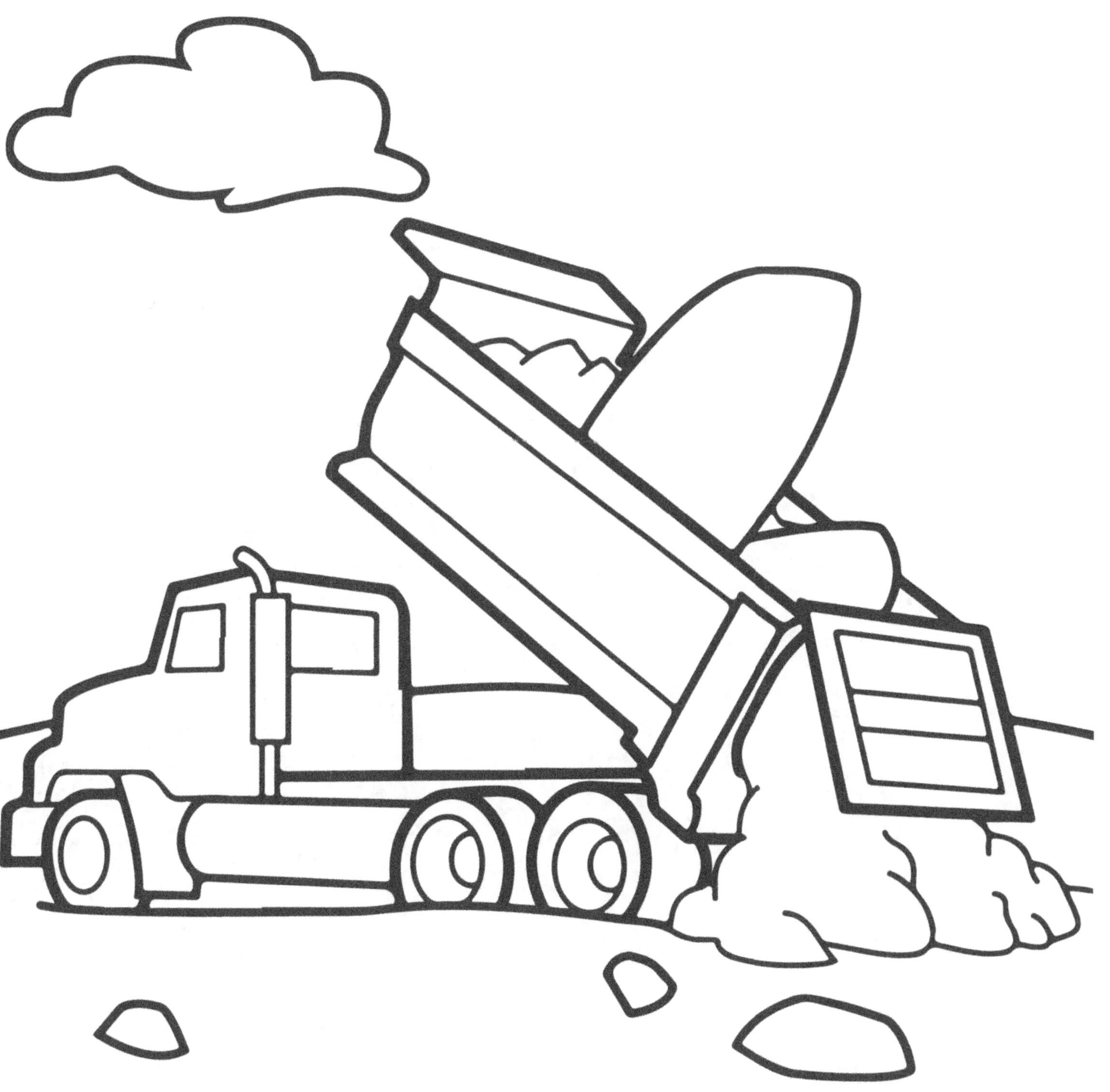

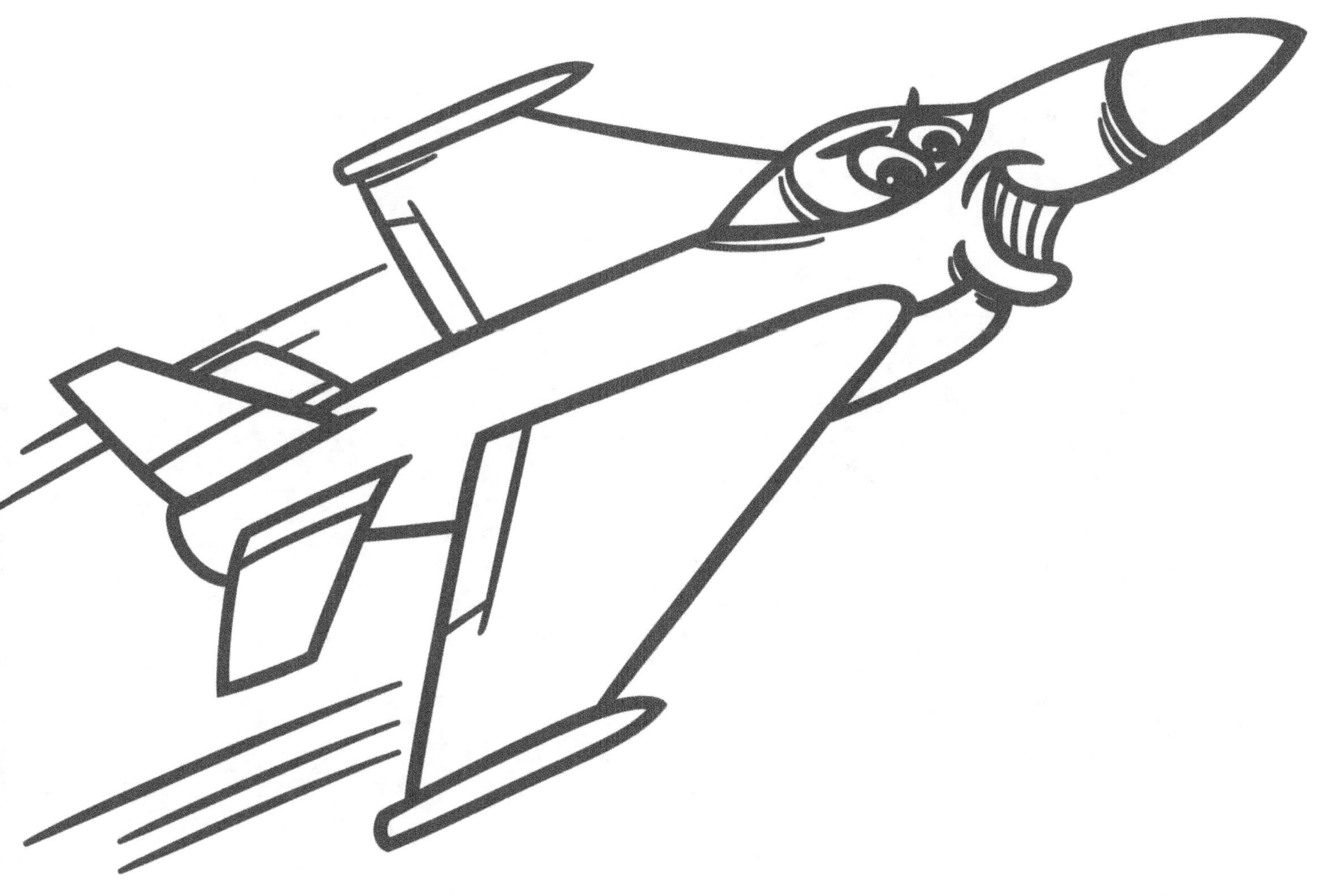

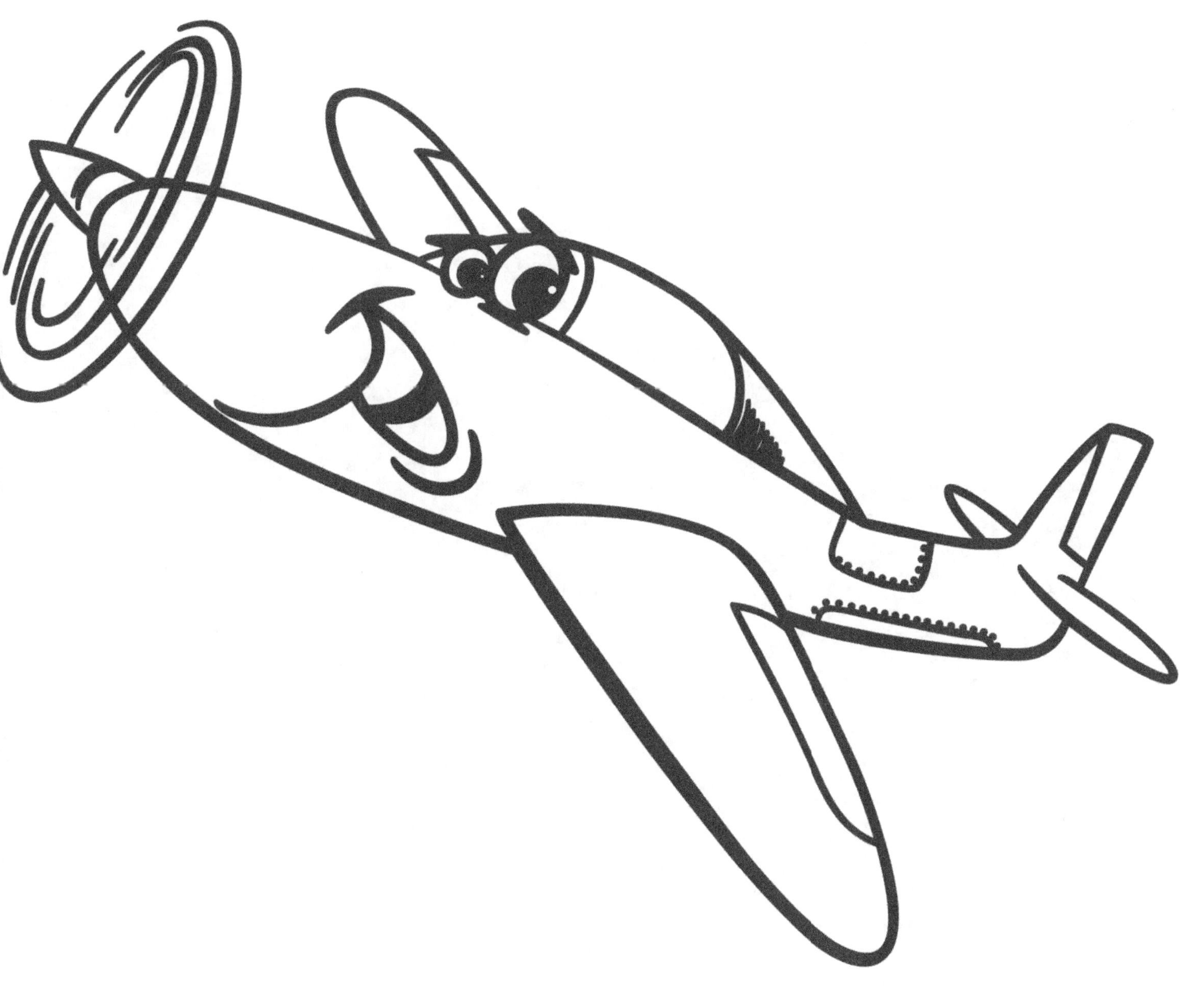

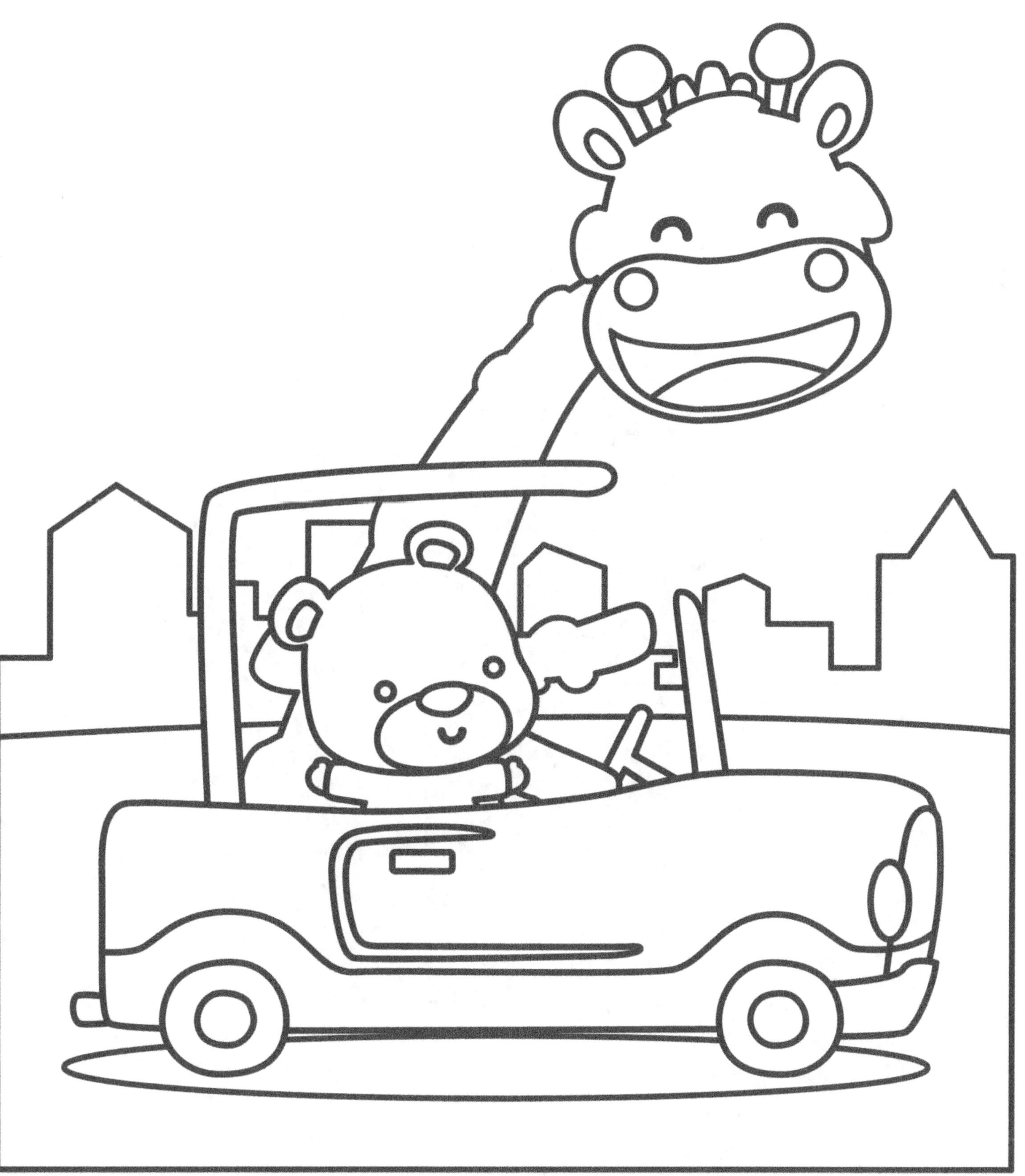

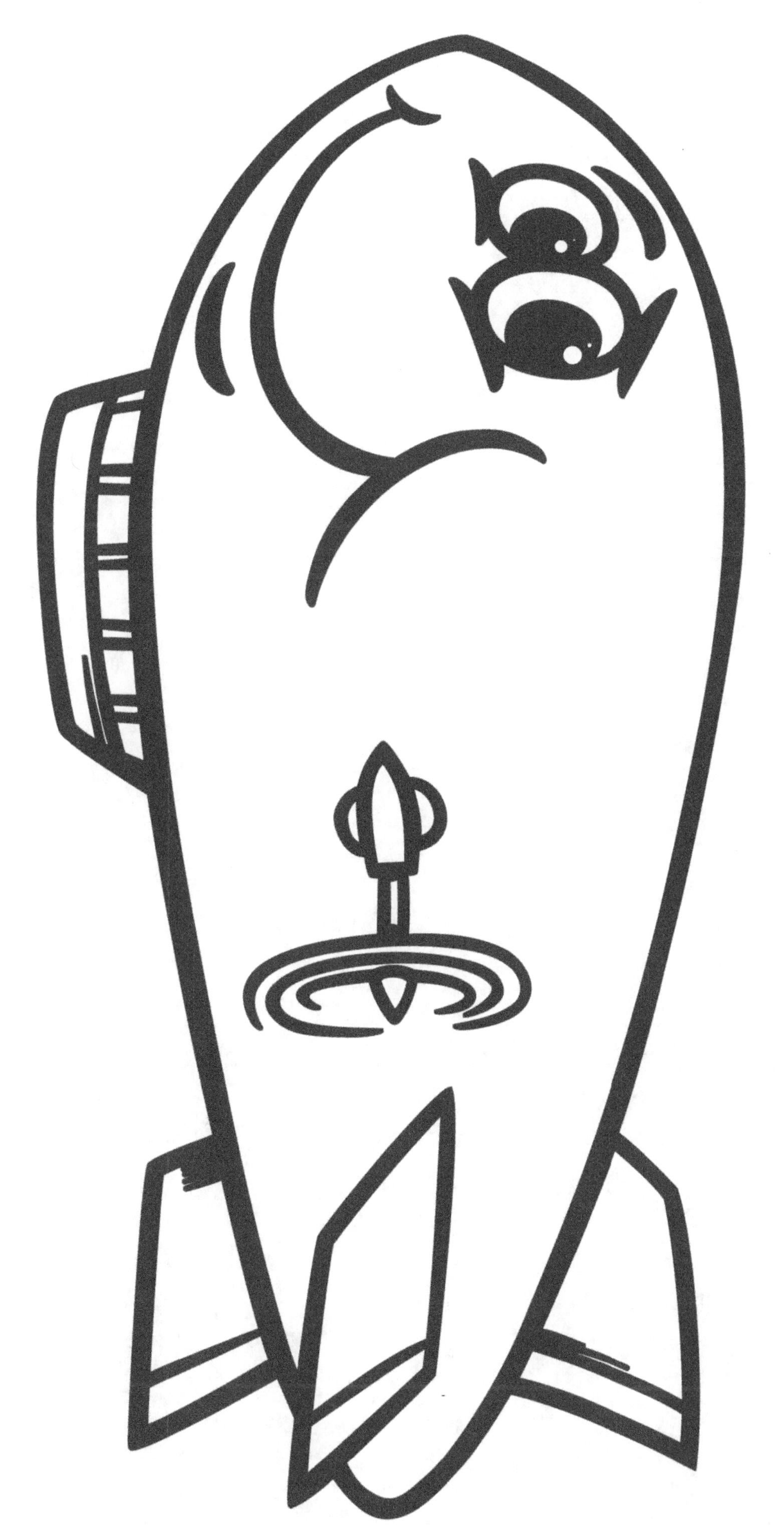

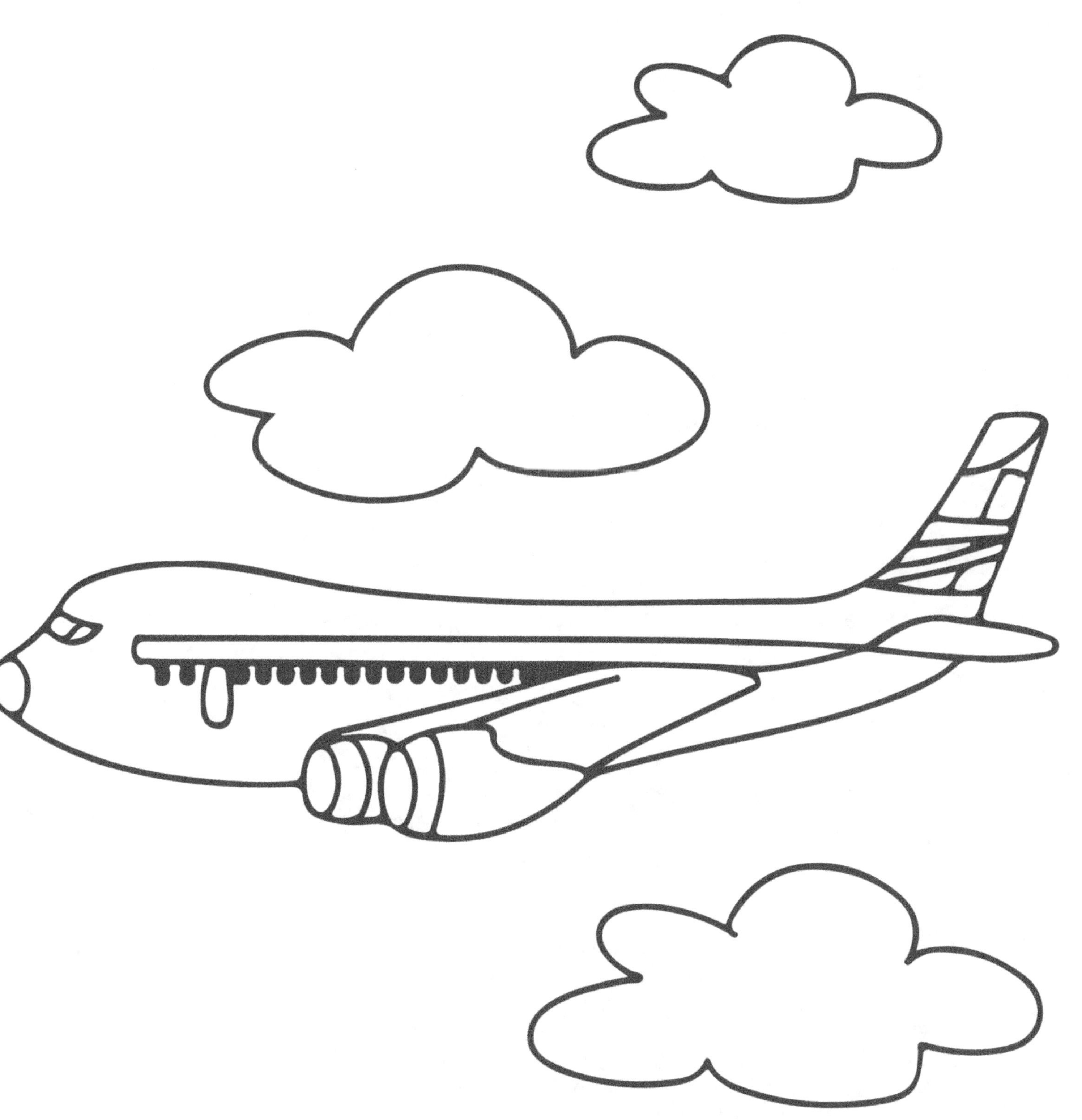